TIMELESS

HYMNS

FOR

FAMILY

WORSHIP

JONI EARECKSON TADA
& BOBBIE WOLGEMUTH

HARVEST HOUSE PUBLISHERS
EUGENE, OREGON

Cover design by Faceout Studio, Lindy Martin
Interior design by Faceout Studio, Paul Nielsen
Artwork by Yuris Yoon
Cover texture © VadimZosimov / Shutterstock

Published in association with the literary agency of Wolgemuth & Associates.

Timeless Hymns for Family Worship
Copyright © 2021 by Joni Eareckson Tada and Robert D. Wolgemuth
Published by Harvest House Publishers
Eugene, Oregon 97408
www.harvesthousepublishers.com

ISBN 978-0-7369-8338-9 (hardcover)
ISBN 978-0-7369-8339-6 (eBook)

Library of Congress Control Number: 2021934270

Printed in China

21 22 23 24 25 26 27 28 29 / RDS / 10 9 8 7 6 5 4 3 2

A Note from Joni About Bobbie Wolgemuth

Look for a moment at the cover of this special book. You'll see the name of my friend and coauthor, Bobbie Wolgemuth. For years, people called Bobbie and me the "hymn ladies." And for a good reason. Every time we got together, we sang the timeless hymns in this book—and many more.

Bobbie and I had such fun putting together this book about our favorite hymns. She and I had learned many by heart when we were kids ourselves! And as adults, we taught these hymns to all the young people we knew. In this book, Bobbie researched and wrote about the history of the hymns (who wrote them and why). I wrote the devotionals (except one, as you'll notice later). We were so excited when this book was first released.

But then my friend was diagnosed with a very serious cancer. During her treatment, Bobbie strengthened her spirit by singing the hymns she had memorized. Several had to do with heaven, and those became her favorites. Whenever she received chemotherapy, Bobbie would come home, put on her sneakers, and walk up and down her neighborhood. As she passed by, neighbors would open their windows to hear her lovely voice.

Bobbie did not survive her battle against cancer. But she was able to keep her bright smile and her strong faith because she trusted Jesus, her Lord and Savior. Did Jesus fail Bobbie because she died? Not at all. It was simply time for her to go home to heaven, and she was satisfied with God's plan. Bobbie Wolgemuth was so content with God's timing that she continued to sing until the day she entered heaven.

I don't know if my friend can peer over the edge of eternity to hear these melodies, but if she is able to, I just bet she's adding lots of harmony.

Thank you, Bobbie, for helping a new generation of boys and girls learn the hymns that you and I treasured for so many years. I'm looking forward to singing with you again in heaven!

CONTENTS

Come, let us sing for joy to the Lord;

let us shout aloud to the Rock of our salvation.

Let us come before him with thanksgiving

and extol him with music and song.

PSALM 95:1-2

Before You Begin

When I was your age, my parents taught me the old hymns of the Christian faith. We sang these hymns around the campfire or while hiking or even at the dinner table after we finished our meal. We sang them so often that I easily memorized all the words.

It was a good thing. When I was a teenager, I dove into shallow water, broke my neck, and became paralyzed. When I learned I'd be in a wheelchair all my life, I felt sad and anxious. But when my family visited me in the hospital, they always cheered me up by singing our favorite hymns!

These hymns comforted me because they reminded me of God's greatness. And they also shared great truths about God and His love for me. After hospital visits were over for the day, I sang these hymns at nighttime when I couldn't sleep. While I sang, I focused on the wonderful themes of trusting God's Word, holding on to His promises, and looking toward heaven. Soon my sadness and anxiety disappeared.

That all happened a long time ago, but I'm still singing all my favorite hymns, and now I'm sharing them with you in this book. You can imagine how happy I am that you now have a chance to sing hymns with your family. I'm hoping you'll sing them so often that you too will learn all the words by heart. And I pray that each word of every hymn will comfort you as it has me!

"HOLY, HOLY, HOLY!"

Always a New Adventure

All of us have grown up with images of heaven in our minds. Whether those images are of golden streets and pearly gates or tropical beaches and peaceful forests, we've all wondered what heaven will actually be like. And even though we may not want to admit it, we've probably secretly wondered if heaven will be a little bit boring. After all, if the worship time in church is limited to twenty minutes of singing, won't we get tired of praising God after a few hundred years?

The Bible says that the seraphim—the big angels that surround God—call out day and night, "Holy, holy, holy!" That's because God is so great and so glorious that no one—not even the highest order of angels—can ever run out of reasons to praise Him. There's always something new to discover about God, which means there will always be something new to discover about heaven. Heaven will be a new adventure every day!

Think of a huge mountain so tall, you could never climb to the top. Or a massive lake so wide, you could never paddle all the way across. Or a sprawling garden where an endless variety of plants and flowers grow. The longer you look and explore and take it all in, the more you realize there is to discover. You will never, ever be able to see it all. I can picture the seraphim catching a glimpse of God from one angle and gasping, "Wow! God is awesome!" But then they see some other aspect of God and shout again, "Whoa, we had no idea You were *this* wonderful, God!"

The seraphim never get tired of proclaiming, "Holy, holy, holy" because God never stops revealing unexpected and breathtaking things about Himself. Moment by moment, He continues to show new aspects of His beauty, His holiness, and His love. Even after spending hundreds of thousands of years in His presence, we will still be discovering new things about Him.

I guarantee you that heaven will never, ever be boring. And even if heaven is not remotely the way you've imagined it, you won't be disappointed. Like the seraphim, you'll never get tired of singing "Holy, holy, holy!" while you worship God. ♫

Reginald Heber grew up in a wealthy English family that had a large library. He loved meeting new people and going new places inside his books. Reginald also loved to read about Jesus and wanted to be like Him—loving and wise.

One year, Reginald wrote a poem that won a top prize in a school contest. After the award ceremony, he went home and into his room. When his mother opened his door, she saw Reginald on his knees telling God how thankful he was that the poem had won first place.

Reginald wanted the verses he wrote to use the best language possible when he talked about God. That's why he says "holy" three times in the first line of "Holy, Holy, Holy." He used the word the Bible says the angels sing when they worship God in heaven.

When we sing "Holy, Holy, Holy!," we say the words the angels do as they take their golden crowns off and place them on the ground in front of Jesus, giving God credit for every good thing in our lives.

HOLY, HOLY, HOLY!

Reginald Heber, 1783–1826 | John B. Dykes, 1823–1876

Ho - ly, ho - ly, ho - ly! Lord God Al - might - y!

Ear - ly in the mor - ing our song shall rise to thee;

Ho - ly, ho - ly, ho - ly! mer - ci - ful and might - y;

God in three per - sons, bless - ed Trin - i - ty!

2)

Holy, holy, holy! All the saints adore Thee,

Casting down their golden crowns around the glassy sea;

Cherubim and seraphim falling down before Thee,

Who wert and art and evermore shalt be.

3)

Holy, holy, holy! Though the darkness hide Thee,

Though the eye of sinful man Thy glory may not see;

Only Thou art holy; there is none beside thee,

Perfect in power, in love, and purity.

4)

Holy, holy, holy! Lord God Almighty!

All Thy works shall praise Thy name in earth and sky and sea;

Holy, holy, holy! Merciful and mighty!

God in three persons, blessed Trinity!

"A MIGHTY FORTRESS IS OUR GOD"

The Power of a Song

Have you ever relied on a song to help you get through something? Maybe you like to listen to music before your soccer game or swim meet. Or you play high-energy tunes when it's time to clean your room or do chores. Singing along to your favorite songs on a family road trip can help the time in the car pass more quickly. Good songs really help!

Once upon a time there was a king named Jehoshaphat whose army was about to go into battle against the enemy. The king was very nervous because the enemy's troops were way stronger—they were better trained and had better weapons. So Jehoshaphat prayed, "God, we don't know what to do, but our eyes are on You."

Do you know what God told King Jehoshaphat to do? He told him to get together a big choir of singers and send them out ahead of the army. *What!* How could this help? Instead of bows and arrows, the choir's only "weapons" were their good singing voices and their trust in God. How in the world would that help win the battle?

Well, it turns out that good songs were powerful here too. The choir marched into battle ahead of the king's army, singing praises to God. And the enemy became totally confused and started fighting against each other. The enemy destroyed their own camp as Jehoshaphat, his troops, and the choir jumped up and down and praised God. What a crazy scene that must have been!

This is why the Bible tells us to sing. Singing God's Word helps us to remember it better. Nobody can ever take away the Bible verses and the songs about God that are in your heart. Whenever you face the enemy—whether the enemy appears as a bully at school or a scary situation or a feeling of fear—you can sing praises to God.

God asks that you trust Him, read the Bible, and sing hymns. When you sing "A Mighty Fortress Is Our God," you are saying that you trust in the Lord. You have the best weapon of all—God's powerful words, which you believe with all of your heart. And with those powerful words, you will always win! ♫

In Germany long ago, people didn't have the Bible in their own language. It was read to them in Latin, but most people couldn't understand it. A boy named Martin Luther was sad that people didn't have Bibles and couldn't sing at church. Only the boys like Martin who knew Latin could be in the church choir, but Martin wanted his friends who spoke only German to be able to sing too.

God gave Martin the wonderful idea to translate the Latin words into German so everyone could read the Bible and sing songs to God in their own language. Martin eventually used his money and talent to print Bibles and hymnbooks. Some people became angry about this and tried to stop him, but that only inspired him to print even more Bibles and hymnbooks. "A Mighty Fortress Is Our God" is one of the hymns he wrote to encourage believers.

Through Martin Luther's courageous work, he guided many people to the Bible, where they would meet God and discover for themselves His mighty words.

A MIGHTY FORTRESS IS OUR GOD

Martin Luther, 1483–1546, translation by Frederick H. Hedge, 1805–1890 | Melody by Martin Luther

A might-y for-tress is our God, A bul-wark nev-er fail - ing; Our
help - er He a - mid the flood Of mor-tal ills pre-vail - ing: For
still our an - cient foe Doth seek to work us woe; His craft and power are
great, And armed with cru - el hate, On earth is not his e - qual.

2)

Did we in our own strength confide, our striving would be losing,

Were not the right man on our side, the man of God's own choosing:

Dost ask who that may be? Christ Jesus, it is He;

Lord Sabaoth, His name, from age to age the same,

And He must win the battle.

3)

And though this world, with devils filled, should threaten to undo us,

We will not fear, for God hath willed His truth to triumph through us:

The prince of darkness grim, we tremble not for him;

His rage we can endure, for lo, his doom is sure;

One little word shall fell him.

4)

That word above all earthly powers, no thanks to them abideth;

The Spirit and the gifts are ours through Him who with us sideth.

Let goods and kindred go, this mortal life also;

The body they may kill: God's truth abideth still;

His kingdom is forever.

"THIS IS MY FATHER'S WORLD"

The God of Incredible Variety

What kind of eater are you? Do you stick with your favorites—peanut butter and jelly sandwiches, spaghetti with your dad's homemade sauce, the same breakfast cereal you eat every morning—or do you love to try new foods?

The other day I had an amazing experience with a new food. My friend held a pear up to my mouth and asked me to take a bite. Now, this wasn't the kind of pear I'm used to eating. Instead of being smooth and yellow or red, it was very large, wrinkled, and almost the color of a peach. It sure didn't look like a pear!

I could have told my friend, "That's a weird-looking pear! No way am I eating that!" But instead I took a bite. And I was so happy I did! I had never tasted anything so sweet before. It smelled almost like perfume, and every mouthful was delicious. "Wow!" I exclaimed. "This tastes great!"

It was my first experience with an Asian pear. As I enjoyed its sweet flavor, my friend reminded me, "God made that. Isn't that neat?" It was more than neat. It was wonderful and amazing. God made Asian pears—along with strawberries and mangoes and apples and every other kind of delicious fruit—to show us how He creates things with incredible variety. He doesn't make just one kind of pear. He makes lots of different kinds of pears. He doesn't make just one kind of flower. He makes thousands of different kinds of flowers. God's magnificent world is made up of so many fantastic shapes and sizes, tastes and colors, aromas and textures—and we get to enjoy them all!

God gives us every single fruit and flower—not to mention a zillion other things—to remind us that He is Lord and Creator of all. He's so imaginative and amazing!

This is His world, and it's filled with His creativity, so you can always find reasons to praise Him. All you need to do is listen and look for all the sounds and sights that show His craftsmanship. When you open your eyes and start seeing the world through your Father's eyes, you will praise Him for the incredible variety He has created as you sing, "This is my Father's world!" ♫

A student in New York had an unusual name and unusual gifts. His name was Maltbie Davenport Babcock, and he was talented in almost everything he did—swimming and baseball and any other sport he tried. Maltbie was also talented in another way. Sensitive and caring, he was fun to be around and liked to laugh, but he always stood up for kids who were being teased or bullied.

A lover of music, Maltbie helped lead a boys' choir and orchestra at school. He also loved nature. Music filled his mind as he walked in the woods and listened to the birds. One day he wrote a hymn called "This Is My Father's World" about the splendor of creation.

Maltbie became a minister and spent his whole life sharing the joy of God. He wanted everyone he met to enjoy all the beautiful things God had made—the mountains, skies, forests, and sea. He was so thrilled to share with others the awesomeness of his Father's world!

THIS IS MY FATHER'S WORLD

Maltbie D. Babcock, 1858–1901 | Franklin L. Sheppard, 1852-1930

2)

This is my Father's world; the birds their carols raise.

The morning light, the lily white, declare their Maker's praise.

This is my Father's world: He shines in all that's fair;

In the rustling grass I hear Him pass; He speaks to me everywhere.

3)

This is my Father's world. O let me ne'er forget

That though the wrong seems oft so strong, God is the Ruler yet.

This is my Father's world: The battle is not done:

Jesus who died shall be satisfied, and earth and heaven be one.

Shout for joy to the LORD, all the earth,
burst into jubilant song with music.

PSALM 98:4

"O FOR A THOUSAND TONGUES TO SING"

Our Forever Home

When I broke my neck many years ago and became paralyzed, I was very sad. The doctors told me I would never walk again. They said I would never be able to use my hands. They told me, "Joni, you'll have to live the rest of your life in a wheelchair." I cried and cried when I heard this news. It seemed like nothing would ever be happy or exciting or fun again.

My friends helped me by visiting me in the hospital. And they *really* helped me by reading the Bible to me. One Bible passage helped a lot. It was 2 Corinthians 4:17-18: "Our light and momentary troubles are achieving for us an eternal glory that far outweighs them all. So we fix our eyes not on what is seen, but on what is unseen, since what is seen is temporary, but what is unseen is eternal."

I might not be able to walk or use my hands again in this world, but someday I will! The Bible lets me know that this world is temporary, but heaven is *forever*. And in that forever world, I will have a brand-new body that can run and jump and do anything I want it to do.

It hasn't always been easy, but as I trust and obey God in my wheelchair, I am preparing myself for my *forever* home in heaven. In that home, I will be joyful and happy—and not just because I can use my arms and legs. I'll be joyful and happy because I will be with Jesus.

The words from the Bible that my friends shared with me helped me when I was feeling sad, and you can use those same words when you're sad or afraid. I love music, so singing my favorite words from the Bible is helpful for me. Those words always make me think of God, and they always make me happy. One of my favorite songs is "O for a Thousand Tongues to Sing." My favorite verse of that song is the last one. It makes me think of all my friends who are blind and deaf who one day will be able to see and hear. And the wonderful last line says, "Leap, ye lame, for joy." That's me! One day I will leap up out of my wheelchair. I can't wait!

Until then, I will continue to obey God here on earth to prepare myself for one day glorifying Him in heaven. And I will keep reading His Word—and *singing* it—to help fear and sadness leave my mind and to add more joy and happiness to my heart. ♫

Charles Wesley had a big family—eighteen brothers and sisters! His mother, Susanna, taught all the children their school lessons at home. They used the Bible as their school textbook and read poetry every day. Soon Charles was writing a lot of poetry, singing the poems he wrote and using them as his prayers.

When Charles was a college student, he gathered with a group of friends every week to talk about the things they were learning in the Bible and to pray for each other. The young men in the group started telling others about God, and Charles started putting Bible verses to music that was easy to learn. This was a great way to teach people more about God's Word.

Charles loved how just saying Jesus's name made fear and worry leave his mind. He encouraged others to sing the words of the Bible when they were afraid too. Charles certainly loved to write poems—he wrote more than a thousand of them! He wanted lots of voices—like the "thousand tongues" of this hymn—to praise God and find comfort in His presence.

O FOR A THOUSAND TONGUES TO SING

Charles Wesley, 1707-1788 | Carl G. Gläser, 1784-1829, arrangement by Lowell Mason, 1792-1872

O for a thou-sand tongues to sing my great Re-deem-er's praise, The

glo-ries of my God and King, the tri-umphs of His grace!

I will sing to the LORD all my life;
I will sing praise to my God as long as I live.

PSALM 104:33

2)

My gracious Master and my God, assist me to proclaim,
To spread through all the earth abroad the honors of Thy name.

3)

Jesus! the name that charms our fears, that bids our sorrows cease,
'Tis music in the sinner's ears, 'tis life and health and peace.

4)

He breaks the power of canceled sin, He sets the prisoner free;
His blood can make the foulest clean; His blood availed for me.

5)

Hear him, ye deaf; His praise, ye dumb, your loosened tongues employ;
Ye blind, behold your Savior come; and leap, ye lame, for joy.

"AMAZING GRACE"

Good Things upon Good Things

Grace. It's a word we hear a lot today. "Just give me some grace." "I'm so grateful for grace." "I owe it all to grace." But what does the word grace actually mean?

We usually see *grace* in the Bible next to words like *justice* and *mercy*, which makes us think that grace has something to do with actions and consequences for those actions. A helpful way to understand the idea of grace is by looking at the relationship between a parent and a child. Children do things—*actions*—and parents respond to those actions with *consequences*.

Right actions usually have positive consequences. But if a child deliberately makes a wrong choice, such as showing unkindness to a sibling or making fun of a friend, the parent needs to give the child a consequence for his or her actions. Children who are disobedient usually receive a punishment, such as a timeout or a loss of privileges. That punishment is *justice*.

Let's say a young child is spending a timeout in her room after saying unkind words to her brother. During the timeout, some relatives stop by unexpectedly to say hello. Instead of being made to stay in her room, the child is allowed to come into the living room to say hi to her relatives and enjoy their visit. Cutting the timeout short is an example of *mercy*. Yes, the child did something wrong, but her parents have chosen not to take a special surprise away from her.

And then the relatives announce that they want to take the family out for ice cream. The parents explain to the child who is supposed to be in a timeout that they aren't rewarding her for being unkind to her brother, but they want her to be able to have fun with her relatives and spend time with them. Yes, she deserves the timeout, but now she's being given *grace*—something good that she didn't do anything to deserve.

As you may have guessed, the child in the story is like us, and her parents are like God. He is consistent in His justice, mercy, and grace. He doesn't turn a blind eye to our actions, and He doesn't hesitate to give us consequences. But He also delights in giving us grace upon grace—good things upon good things—that we don't always deserve. And *that's* pretty amazing! ♫

There once lived a boy in England who helped change the world. His name was John Newton. His mother died when he was only seven years old, and he was sent to a boarding school. When he was eleven, he began to travel with his father, who was a sea captain on a merchant ship. Eventually, John became a ship captain himself. But sadly, he did not sell things like ivory, gold, wood, or beeswax. Instead, John sold men and women into slavery.

But God was about to change John's heart. Something began to stir in him, and he started reading the Bible. With every page he read, John started to see that what he was doing to the slaves was sinful and wrong. He decided to stop selling slaves and instead obey God's voice.

John gave up being a ship captain and studied to be a minister. He admitted to everyone that he had done terrible things, but God had forgiven him. He wrote the hymn "Amazing Grace" because he was so thankful that God had forgiven him and changed his heart.

AMAZING GRACE

John Newton, 1725-1807 | Early American melody, arrangement by Edwin O. Excell, 1821-1921

A - maz - ing grace! How sweet the sound That saved a wretch like me! I once was lost, but now am found, Was blind, but now I see.

2)

'Twas grace that taught my heart to fear,
And grace my fears relieved;
How precious did that grace appear
The hour I first believed!

3)

Through many dangers, toils, and snares,
I have already come;
'Tis grace hath brought me safe thus far,
And grace will lead me home.

4)

When we've been there ten thousand years,
Bright shining as the sun,
We've no less days to sing God's praise
Than we we'd first begun.

"TO GOD BE THE GLORY"

Giving All the Praise to God

I've always loved to read stories about people who praised God no matter what. One person I've always admired is Corrie ten Boom. Corrie was a Christian who lived in Holland and was such a strong believer in following Jesus, she risked her own life to protect her Jewish friends and neighbors during World War II. The Nazis caught her, though, and threw her into prison.

After the war was over, Corrie was released from the concentration camp. She was so grateful to God for the way He had protected her from the horrors of the camp. She started traveling all over the world to tell people about God's love and forgiveness. Many people came to know her story, and Corrie became famous for her strong faith in Jesus.

Whenever she spoke at big churches, people crowded around her and said, "Oh, what a great saint of God you are," or "I'm amazed you were able to forgive the Nazi soldiers who beat you when you were in the concentration camp." These people were very kind, but Corrie felt a little embarrassed. They were putting her on a pedestal, and she felt uncomfortable with that. She had never wanted people to be amazed by her—that wasn't why she had protected Jewish people. She had simply done what Jesus had asked her to do, and she wanted Him to have all the glory.

Tired of hearing people praise her instead of God, Corrie came up with a plan. Patiently, she listened to the wonderful things people said to her, accepting each compliment as though it were a rosebud. She gathered many blessings that way, just like gathering a beautiful bouquet of flowers. Every evening she remembered all the nice things people had said about her and presented all those compliments as a big bouquet of praise to God. She would say, "Lord Jesus, this person was amazed I could forgive, but You are the one who forgave the most when You were on the cross." Or, "Lord Jesus, a person told me today that she thought I was a great Christian, but there are no great Christians—only a great Savior."

Corrie pointed others to Jesus as the source of her joy and positivity, and she praised Jesus for every good thing that had happened to her. She believed what the hymn says: "To God be the glory." All the praise and compliments she received were because of God, and she offered them back to Him with a smiling face and a thankful heart. ♫

Once there was a sweet blind girl named Fanny Crosby. Even though she lived her whole life in the dark, she kept smiling. Fanny loved taking long walks with her grandmother in the field around their farmhouse, smelling the meadow flowers, dangling her feet in the trickling brook, listening to the birds singing, and feeling the wind through the trees. Her grandmother also read lots of books to Fanny, including great classic books, poetry, and the Bible. Repeating the words her grandmother read, Fanny learned to memorize huge portions of the Bible.

When she was eleven, Fanny prayed, "Dear Lord, please show me how I can learn like other children." The next year, her prayer was answered when she was accepted into the New York Institute for the Blind. At the new school, Fanny learned to play the organ, piano, guitar, and harp, and she excelled as the top student in music, literature, history, and languages.

Fanny wrote over nine thousand poems in her life. One of those poems was "To God Be the Glory," which she wrote to tell everyone that God is the one who answered her prayers and dreams.

TO GOD BE THE GLORY

Fanny J. Crosby, 1820-1915 | William H. Doane, 1832-1915

To God be the glo-ry, great things He hath done, So loved He the

world that He gave us His Son, Who yield-ed His life an a-tone-ment for

sin, And o-pened the Life-gate that all may go in. Praise the

Lord, praise the Lord, let the earth hear His voice! Praise the Lord, praise the Lord, let the

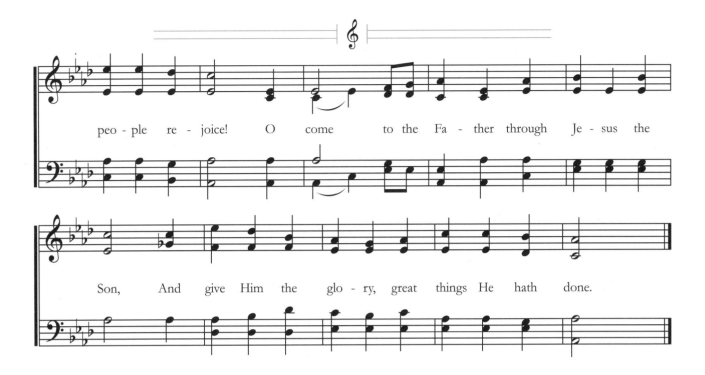

peo - ple re - joice! O come to the Fa - ther through Je - sus the

Son, And give Him the glo - ry, great things He hath done.

2)

O perfect redemption, the purchase of blood,

To every believer the promise of God;

The vilest offender who truly believes,

That moment from Jesus a pardon receives.

Refrain

Praise the Lord, praise the Lord, let the earth hear His voice!

Praise the Lord, praise the Lord, let the people rejoice!

O come to the Father, through Jesus the Son,

And give Him the glory, great things He hath done.

3)

Great things He has taught us, great things He has done,

And great our rejoicing through Jesus the Son;

But purer, and higher, and greater will be

Our wonder, our transport, when Jesus we see.

Refrain

"PRAISE TO THE LORD, THE ALMIGHTY"

Every Good Thing

When I'm feeling sad or discouraged, two things always help me feel better: God and my friends. I remember one of those days when I was feeling really down. It was a boring Saturday afternoon, I was feeling super uncomfortable sitting in my wheelchair, and I was even having trouble breathing. Something had to change, so I came up with a plan. Whenever I breathed hard, instead of complaining, I would say out loud, "The Lord is good."

My friend was sitting with me, after hearing me say "The Lord is good" about five times, she turned and laughingly rolled her eyes at me. "What are you doing, Joni?" she asked. "Trying to convince yourself the Lord is good?"

"You've got it," I replied as we both smiled. It's not that I doubted God's goodness on that boring, discouraging Saturday. I just had to keep reminding myself of the truth—out loud, with my friend listening.

King David in the Bible did exactly the same thing. Whenever he was feeling sad, he would say to himself, "Why, my soul, are you downcast? Why so disturbed within me? Put your hope in God, for I will yet praise him, my Savior and my God" (Psalm 42:5-6).

I want to be like King David. I want to praise God all the time. When I feel happy and when I feel sad. When I'm busy with fun things to do and when I'm bored with nothing to do. When I'm with my friends and when I'm alone by myself. I need to remind myself with the words to our hymn today: "O my soul, praise Him, for He is thy health and salvation!" It's easy to say God is good when you're feeling great. But it's another thing—a much harder thing—to say (and sing) out loud that God is good when you're feeling unhappy.

Every good thing comes from God. That's important to remember. And it's also important to remember to praise God for every good thing. A best friend. A sunny day. Even a rainy day. Most of all, you can praise God for who He is—an amazing, great, and powerful friend. The next time you're feeling a little sad, try talking to your soul. You can even use the words to "Praise to the Lord, the Almighty" to remind yourself of all the wonderful things about God. Tell a friend. Tell your family. Tell yourself. And especially tell God! 🎵

In Germany long ago there lived a stubborn and rebellious young man named Joachim Neander. One day Joachim and his friends heard that a famous preacher was coming to town. They planned to pretend to listen to him and then make fun of what he said. But something amazing happened. Instead of tricking the preacher, Joachim was touched by the message. He asked God to forgive him, and he asked Jesus to be his Savior. He changed his ways and followed God's path.

One of the first things Joachim did was find new friends who followed Jesus. He also began listening to concert music and became inspired to write down the words he felt in his heart.

Because God's message had changed his heart when he was young, Joachim Neander grew up to give the world a glorious poem—"Praise to the Lord, the Almighty." He knew that the best way to say thank you to God was to praise Him for being such an amazing, great, and powerful friend!

PRAISE TO THE LORD, THE ALMIGHTY

Joachim Neander, 1650-1680, translation by Catherine Winkworth, 1827-1878 | John B. Dykes, 1823–1876

Praise to the Lord, the Al - might-y, the King of cre - a - tion!

O my soul, praise Him, for He is thy health and sal - va - tion!

All ye who hear, now to His tem - ple draw near;

Join me in glad ad - o - ra - tion!

2)

Praise to the Lord, who o'er all things so wondrously reigneth,

Shelters thee under His wings, yea, so gently sustaineth!

Hast thou not seen how thy desires e'er have been

Granted in what He ordaineth?

3)

Praise to the Lord, who doth prosper thy work and defend thee;

Surely His goodness and mercy here daily attend thee.

Ponder anew what the Almighty can do,

If with His love He befriend thee.

4)

Praise to the Lord, O let all that is in me adore Him!

All that hath life and breath, come now with praises before Him.

Let the Amen sound from His people again,

Gladly for aye we adore Him.

"FAIREST LORD JESUS"

Ruler of All Creation

I have always loved the outdoors. When I was a kid, my family liked to sit in the backyard during the summer and watch the sun go down. "There it goes," my sister Kathy would say. "There's just a little tip of light left—see it?" My sisters and I would each try to be the last one to see the sun set. It was fun to watch the sun go down, the colors in the sky fade, and the stars begin to shine. After it became dark, my dad would often light a fire in the backyard pit, and he'd lead us in singing hymns.

As we were singing, we would count the constellations. "Who can find the Big Dipper?" Daddy would ask.

"Over there!" My sister Jay would jump to her feet and point.

"And Orion?"

"I see it, I see it!" someone would say.

"Who knows a hymn about the sun and stars?" Daddy would ask. We would scratch our heads, trying hard to think of a hymn that talked about nature.

"Let me give you a hint," Daddy would say. "Fairest Lord Jesus, Ruler of all…" He'd stretch out his sentence, waiting for us to guess the next word.

"I know, I know!" we'd chime in and start singing about Jesus being greater than the woodlands, the sunshine and moonlight, and all the twinkling, starry host. We loved singing that song as we sat around the fire, looking into the night sky God had created.

Have you ever wondered why God made waterfalls and sandy beaches and sparkling lakes? He made them to show us what He is like. He made the sun and the moon to show us He's the light of the world. He made the woodlands with big, tall trees to show us His towering strength. He created the flowers and fruits and vegetables. He even made the four seasons—spring, summer, fall, and winter—to show us the variety of His beauty and splendor.

Jesus is Ruler of all creation. He is fairer and purer than anything or anybody we can imagine. Best of all, He shares all of creation with us. We can see it and feel it and experience it. That's something to sing about! ♫

Very long ago in Germany, many Christians were being hunted down and put in prison. These believers called themselves "the Brotherhood" because they were like a big family. They loved God, and they sang all the time. They sang so much that they became known as "the singing Brethren." Their leader, John Hus, had been put in prison, and even there he continued singing. In fact, the last sound his friends heard from him was his voice singing a hymn.

The singing Brethren's enemies thought they had stopped the message of Jesus from being spread. But the good news didn't stop. Meeting in secret places, they sang together and encouraged each other to keep their faith in God strong. When they felt sad or alone, they sang hymns like "Fairest Lord Jesus."

Many years later, a visitor came to one of the German villages. He heard some children singing "Fairest Lord Jesus." Quickly he wrote down the words and memorized the tune, and in no time the song was on the lips of children all over the world.

FAIREST LORD JESUS

Anonymous | Based on a folk tune

Fair - est Lord Je - sus, rul - er of all na - ture, O Thou of

God and man the Son, Thee will I cher - ish,

Thee will I hon - or, Thou, my soul's glo - ry joy, and crown.

2)

Fair are the meadows, fairer still the woodlands,
Robed in the blooming garb of spring:
Jesus is fairer, Jesus is purer,
Who makes the woeful heart to sing.

3)

Fair is the sunshine, fairer still the moonlight,
And all the twinkling starry host:
Jesus shines brighter, Jesus shines purer
Than all the angels heaven can boast.

4)

Beautiful Savior! Lord of the nations!
Son of God and Son of Man!
Glory and honor, praise, adoration
Now and forevermore be Thine!

"WHEN WE ALL GET TO HEAVEN"

Going Back Home

You know that feeling you get when you've been gone for a while and finally come back home? Maybe you've been to away to camp, and it feels so good to be back in your own comfy bed. Or you've been visiting your grandparents in another state, and it's great to see your family and friends back home again. You can even get that coming-home feeling after you've been playing at a friend's house for the day and you come home to your favorite meal of pasta and homemade bread.

One of my favorite memories as a little girl was playing late-afternoon tag in the woods beyond our backyard with my sister Kathy and our neighborhood friends. When we called to each other, our shouts echoed through the tall oak trees. Other sounds echoed too—the chatter of birds, the buzz of a lawn mower up the street, the sound of garage doors opening as parents came home from work. Our play was so much fun that an hour would go by and we'd hardly know it.

Finally my sister and my friends and I would hear our parents calling us home for dinner. Hearing their voices made me so happy, I would almost start to cry. Maybe it was anticipating the fried chicken and mashed potatoes waiting for us at home. Or maybe it was knowing that as a part of the family, I had my very own special place at the dinner table. Mostly I think I just enjoyed the simple idea of going home. Home was a place where I was welcomed, where I was loved, where I belonged. More than that, I knew my family wasn't complete without me—and *that* made me feel needed and wanted and loved. Home was place where I *fit*.

Just like my parents made our house feel like home, Jesus is preparing a special place for us in heaven. He might not be serving fried chicken and mashed potatoes (or maybe He will!), but no matter how different heaven is from my home here on earth, I know it's a place where I'll feel welcomed and where I'll fit. And you will feel just as welcomed there too! We will live in the brightest, most wonderful home ever. As crazy as it sounds, heaven simply wouldn't be complete without you and me. When we all get to heaven, we'll all have a place at God's table. When we all see Jesus, we'll sing and shout, "We're home!" ♫

Cheerful Eliza Hewitt loved school as a child and decided to become a schoolteacher. But one day something terrible and unexpected happened to Eliza while she was teaching school. A student who had been misbehaving hit her with a heavy piece of slate. Eliza's back was terribly injured, and she had to be put in a body cast. Even though she couldn't walk or run, Eliza busied herself with memorizing poetry and singing. When she started feeling sorry for herself, she made herself stop and count her blessings. It took six months for Eliza to heal, but on the day the doctor removed her cast, she was so happy that she threw a party for all her friends!

Eliza often thought about how splendid heaven must be. She imagined how people who were sick or crippled would one day be free from pain and running on heaven's streets of gold. She pictured the big party that was being prepared in heaven, and she wrote a poem about the big day—"When We All Get to Heaven."

WHEN WE ALL GET TO HEAVEN

Eliza E. Hewitt, 1851-1920 | John B. Dykes, 1823–1876

Sing the won-drous love of Je-sus, sing His mer-cy and His grace;

In the man-sions bright and bless-ed, He'll pre-pare for us a place. When we

all get to heav-en, what a day of re-joic-ing that will be! When we

all see Je-sus, we'll sing and shout the vic-to-ry!

2)

While we walk the pilgrim pathway, clouds will overspread the sky;
But when traveling days are over, not a shadow, not a sigh.

Refrain

When we all get to heaven, what a day of rejoicing that will be!
When we all see Jesus, we'll sing and shout the victory!

3)

Let us then be true and faithful, trusting, serving every day;
Just one glimpse of Him in glory will the toils of life repay.

Refrain

4)

Onward to the prize before us! Soon His beauty we'll behold;
Soon the pearly gates will open; we shall tread the streets of gold.

Refrain

"HOW FIRM A FOUNDATION"

The Strongest Support

I was raised on a farm that had a big red barn surrounded by weeping willows. My father was very proud of the old barn—it had stood for more than a hundred years. The stones in the foundation had been gathered from the fields and along the stream, and each stone was very large and heavy. The foundation was thick and sank deep into the earth. It's a good thing the foundation was strong—it had to support a barn full of hay, feed, tractors, and other farm equipment.

One night we were awakened by horses' whinnying and shouts from neighbors. Our barn was on fire! The fire trucks arrived, but it was too late. The big red barn and all the hay and machinery burned to the ground. Fortunately, all the animals were safe, but the next day I sadly watched my father sort through the smoking ruins, looking for bits and pieces of his favorite tools. Nothing was left. Then he walked up to the foundation and ran his hands over the stones, which were still warm. He took a hammer and tapped the foundation. Then he stepped back and announced it had survived the fire. It was strong enough to carry the weight of a new barn. The next day my dad began building on that foundation.

My family was able to build a new barn because the original foundation was so strong. Soon we had a brand-new home for our horses and other animals and farm equipment. We were able to take a bad situation and make it better than ever. That's what happens when you have a strong foundation!

Sometimes bad things happen, and it seems like everything has gone up in smoke. But thankfully, if we are followers of Jesus, we have a strong foundation in our lives—a foundation much stronger than anything that can support a barn or a house. That strong foundation keeps us strong too. We can overcome anything with Jesus in our lives!

God gives us strength in His Word, the Bible. It's the foundation of every Christian's life. By singing words from the Bible—like the words in "How Firm a Foundation"—you can be bold and courageous for God. You can take a bad situation and make it better. You can sing when you're scared, and God's words will help you feel brave and strong. The next time you are sad or afraid, remember that God is your firm foundation that nothing can destroy. When you build your life on the strongest foundation, you can overcome anything! ♫

Do you have a special collection? Like rocks or shells from the beach or stuffed animals or T-shirts from places you've traveled? Maybe your mom or dad collects books or coffee mugs or antiques. Collecting things is fun!

A young man in London, England, had a very special collection. His name was John Rippon, and he collected hymns. When he was in college, John decided to hunt for the very best hymns he could find and put them in a book.

John selected "How Firm a Foundation" for his hymn collection because it is filled with great truth. Some of the people who sang this song were facing very hard times. They were tired and discouraged. This hymn helped them to be brave. Whether out loud or silently in their heads, they could sing the words all day and remember that God would help them. The smallest children could sing even if they couldn't read. John Rippon's collection made a difference by helping people put God's Word in their hearts.

HOW FIRM A FOUNDATION

From John Rippon's "Selection of Hymns," 1787 | Early American melody

How firm a foun - da - tion, ye saints of the Lord, Is laid for your

faith in His ex - cel - lent Word! What more can He say than to You He hath

said, To you who for ref - uge to Je - sus have fled?

2)

"Fear not, I am with thee; O be not dismayed,

For I am thy God, and will still give thee aid;

I'll strengthen thee, help thee, and cause thee to stand,

Upheld by my righteous, omnipotent hand.

3)

"When through fiery trials thy pathway shall lie,

My grace, all-sufficient, shall be thy supply;

The flame shall not hurt thee; I only design

Thy dross to consume, and thy gold to refine.

4)

"The soul that on Jesus still leans for repose,

I will not, I will not desert to his foes;

That soul, though all hell should endeavor to shake,

I'll never, no, never, no, never forsake!"

"TAKE MY LIFE, AND LET IT BE"

I Can Sing!

Do you love to sing? Ever since I was a little girl, I've loved making melodies and singing my favorite songs. I could sing anywhere—at home, in church, with my friends, in the car…anywhere at all!

After the diving accident in which I became paralyzed, my parents worried that I had lost the use of my body. They begged a specialist to come to the hospital to examine me. The expert stood by my bedside and began poking my feet and ankles with a pin, trying to find out what I could feel. He slowly poked his way up my legs asking, "Can you feel this?" and I would shake my head no. "This?" and again I would say no. He reached my waist and then my chest, and *still* I couldn't feel anything. I panicked. I was desperate to show him that I could do *something*. So when I still couldn't feel a pinprick at my collarbone level, I blurted out, "I can't feel that, but…but I can sing! Wanna hear me? Really, I can!" I then burst into song.

I've been singing ever since. I can't do a lot physically. Because of my injury, I can't use my hands. That means I can't hold things, and I don't have very much strength in my arms. I can't walk or run. But I *can* sing, and that's why I love this special hymn, "Take My Life, and Let It Be." I may be in a wheelchair, but I can still do a whole lot of things for God. I can pray and be loyal and patient, considerate and generous. I can encourage others and be a good friend. I can help other disabled people through my ministry. But most of all, I can sing praises to God.

Even when life is hard, I love to rejoice. I always feel better when I choose to praise God instead of complaining about the things I can't do. I may not be able to change a lot of things, but I can change the way I feel about those things. I can choose to focus on the things I can't do, or I can choose to focus on the things I *can* do. Like singing. And I can choose to do those things well and do them with a joyful spirit.

Sometimes other people can bring our mood down. But you can still keep your joyful spirit, and you can help others too. When you are around someone who focuses on what they can't do, you can pray for them. You can pray the words from this hymn for them and also for yourself. It will be fun to see what blessing God sends to them—and to you. There's a good chance that both of you will end up singing and smiling and praising God!

A girl named Frances Ridley Havergal had a wonderful treasure. It wasn't a toy or a piece of jewelry—it was a treasure inside her heart. From the time she was very small, Frances could sing like a beautiful songbird. When Frances was only seven years old, she began to write verses. She also studied piano and played and sang at concerts.

Everyone loved to be around Frances because she was so cheerful and happy. Do you know why? It's really very simple. She prayed for everyone around her. As she played with her friends or talked to adults, she secretly asked God to work in their lives.

One day Frances went on vacation and noticed that some of the people with her were very grumpy. So she prayed that God would give everyone in the house a blessing. He did, and soon everyone was smiling and positive! Frances was so happy she couldn't sleep, and that night she wrote the poem "Take My Life and Let It Be." God gave Frances a treasure, and she shared that treasure with others.

"TAKE MY LIFE, AND LET IT BE"

Francis R. Havergal, 1836-1879 | H.A. César Malan, 1787-1864

Take my life, and let it be con - se - crat - ed, Lord, to Thee;

Take my hands, and let them move at the im - pulse

of Thy love, At the im - pulse of Thy love.

2)

Take my feet, and let them be swift and beautiful for Thee;
Take my voice, and let me sing always, only for my King,
Always, only for my King.

3)

Take my lips, and let them be filled with messages for Thee;
Take my silver and my gold; not a mite would I with-hold,
Not a mite would I with-hold.

4)

Take my love, my God, I pour at Thy feet its treasure store;
Take myself and I will be ever, only, all for Thee,
Ever, only, all for Thee.

"NOTHING BUT THE BLOOD OF JESUS"

New Life Forever

Did you know that there is something inside your body that you cannot live without? Your heart pumps it every second. It carries nourishment throughout your body. It fights infection and helps heal wounds. Even though you rarely see it, it gives you energy and keeps you healthy. Have you guessed what it is? It's blood.

You probably don't think about your blood as it does its amazing work inside your body all day and all night. In fact, you might think about your blood only when you skin your knee or elbow and need to clean the wound and put a bandage on it so it stops bleeding. Or if you have to get your blood drawn at the doctor's office, which is something that scares a lot of us. But blood is really important! You need it to live. God created blood, and He has been teaching people something important about it from the beginning of time.

Do you remember way back in the Bible when God created Adam and Eve? Do you remember how they chose to disobey God in the Garden of Eden? Satan, the serpent, tricked them into eating some fruit that God had told them never to eat, and after that, sin came into Adam and Eve's world. To cover the cost of that sin, the blood of an innocent animal had to be shed. And that continued to happen throughout the Old Testament.

When Jesus came into the world and died on the cross for our sins, He paid for every awful thing everyone had ever done—and every awful thing everyone in the future would do. His blood washed our sins away. And that's why the hymn "Nothing but the Blood of Jesus" is so powerful. With the blood of Jesus, God announces to you and me, "You can be clean from your sins forever!"

Blood is so important for life! And the blood of Jesus covers our sins and gives us new life. His blood makes us strong. Everybody needs it. It will make us clean inside…forever. You don't have to be afraid of seeing this blood. You don't have to be scared or grossed out by it. It's something to celebrate because it shows how much Jesus loves you and how He has washed away your sins forever. ♪

As a young child, Robert Lowry challenged himself to play every musical instrument he could get his hands on. Music was always running through his mind, and he composed melodies and jotted down lyrics on the margins of newspapers, the backs of envelopes, and any other scrap of paper he could find.

Seeking to learn more about God, Lowry joined First Baptist Church of Philadelphia when he was seventeen. where he started teaching Sunday school and singing in the choir. He soon decided to become a preacher, and besides studying the Bible, Lowry also organized a college choir and taught music to his fellow students.

While Lowry always said he preferred preaching sermons to writing hymns, he was a gifted hymn writer who wrote many songs we still sing today. One of those hymns, "Nothing but the Blood of Jesus," was first sung by groups at a camp meeting by the ocean in New Jersey. People came to the meeting to worship God while they escaped the summer heat of the cities—and they were encouraged as they were reminded to put their faith and trust in Jesus.

"NOTHING BUT THE BLOOD OF JESUS"

Robert Lowry, 1826-1899　|　Robert Lowry

What can wash a - way my sin? Noth-ing but the blood of Je - sus;

What can make me whole a - gain? No-thing but the blood of Je - sus.

Oh! pre - cious is the flow that makes me white as snow!

No oth - er fount I know, noth-ing but the blood of Je - sus.

2)

For my pardon this I see: nothing but the blood of Je-sus!
For my cleansing, this my plea: nothing but the blood of Jesus.

Refrain

Oh! precious is the flow that makes me white as snow!
No other fount I know, nothing but the blood of Jesus.

3)

Nothing can for sin atone, nothing but the blood of Jesus;
Naught of good that I have done, nothing but the blood of Jesus.

Refrain

4)

This is all my hope and peace: nothing but the blood of Jesus;
This is all my righteousness: nothing but the blood of Jesus.

Refrain

"WHEN I SURVEY THE WONDROUS CROSS"

The Very Best Friend

This special story was written by Bobbie, my friend who went to heaven. I didn't want to change it because it contains an important lesson on how God can use you to reach your friends for Jesus!

When I was a little girl, I had everything that most children would ever dream of owning. I lived in a big red brick house in a really nice town, and I went swimming, played tennis, and rode my bike wherever I liked. I took piano lessons and had many talents, and a lot of people would probably say my life was pretty close to perfect. But I was often sad on the inside. I sometimes felt lonely, and I even did some mean things to other kids when adults weren't watching.

I had a friend named Martha who lived across the street from me. Martha didn't have fancy clothes or tons of toys like me, but she had something I didn't have—a close family who spent lots of time with her. I loved to go to Martha's house and play with her baby sister and sing songs beside their plain brown piano in the corner of the playroom.

One day, Martha's family invited me to church. I put on my prettiest dress and scrunched into the back seat of the car next to Martha. Inside the church building, notes boomed out from the organ pipes, and everyone stood to sing like one huge choir. I was given my very own Bible, and I learned that Jesus could live in my heart and help me have a happier life. Martha's mom explained to me that I could ask Jesus to forgive me for all the mean things I'd said and done, and I prayed and asked Jesus into my heart right then and there.

That prayer changed my life! I didn't have a perfect life from then on, but I *did* have a new best friend named Jesus who would help me when I felt sad or lonely. Pretty soon, others began to notice that I had changed. I was happy and content and didn't feel like I needed to be mean to others. Instead, I wanted to be nice to them. I wasn't scared or sad or lonely anymore.

Now whenever I look at the cross, I see Jesus, and I know how much He loves me. I see the light of His love, and I am determined to share that love with everyone I meet. I'm so thankful that Martha and her family introduced me to Jesus, and I'm so glad He came into my heart that day. ♫

Nobody could argue that young Isaac Watts had a gift for languages. He learned Latin at age four, Greek at nine, French at eleven, and Hebrew at thirteen. Born in England and the oldest of eight children, Isaac spent much of his time thinking and studying. His physical body was never strong, but he had a brilliant mind.

Isaac's father was a pastor, and Isaac often complained that the only hymns they sang in church were taken from the Old Testament book of Psalms. He longed to sing about the New Testament good news of Jesus coming to earth to die for our sins. His father, weary of Isaac's complaining, challenged him to write something different. Isaac took his father's challenge to heart and spent his life writing words to hymns—more than seven hundred of them!

One of those hymns, "When I Survey the Wondrous Cross," has been called "the greatest hymn in the English language." It celebrates the life of Christ and encourages believers with the good news of His death and resurrection.

"WHEN I SURVEY THE WONDROUS CROSS"

Isaac Watts, 1674-1748 | Plainchant melody, arrangement by Lowell Mason, 1792-1872

2)

Forbid it, Lord, that I should boast,
Save in the death of Christ, my God;
All the vain things that charm me most,
I sacrifice them to His blood.

3)

See, from His head, His hands, His feet,
Sorrow and love flow mingled down;
Did e'er such love and sorrow meet,
Or thorns compose so rich a crown?

4)

Were the whole realm of nature mine,
That were a present far too small;
Love so amazing, so divine,
Demands my soul, my life, my all.

"CROWN HIM WITH MANY CROWNS"

An A-Plus from God

Did you ever dress up as a prince or a princess when you were little? If you did, you might have worn a crown. And that crown transformed you into royalty!

God wants to give you a crown of your own—and you don't have to pretend to be a prince or a princess to wear it, because you already are one! We might imagine a crown studded with pearls and diamonds, but this crown will be even better than that. It will be a heavenly crown. The Bible talks about this special crown: "Now there is in store for me the crown of righteousness, which the Lord, the righteous Judge, will award to me on that day—and not only to me, but also to all who have longed for his appearing" (2 Timothy 4:8).

Isn't it amazing that God wants to reward you with a crown? It will be even better than an A-plus on a test or a gold medal. Won't it be wonderful to know that you've lived a life that really pleases God? Won't it be great to feel His approval when He presents you with a real crown? In fact, depending on how much you choose to follow God here on earth, there may be *several* crowns waiting for you in heaven.

What's extra amazing about these crowns is that they won't be all about us. We will be able to share these rewards with God and give them back to Him. Because we are nothing without our heavenly Father. He made us, and every good thing in our lives comes from Him. That's why after we receive our crown (or even crowns!), we will want to give them back to Him and, like the hymn says, "crown Him with many crowns."

Just imagine the moment. You'll be standing with believers from Africa and Asia and Europe and places all over the world, all holding crowns. And then as Jesus rises to the throne, you will give your crowns—and all glory—back to Him. Crowns of praise and honor, glory and greatness. I can't think of a better way to honor Jesus and to thank Him for all He has done! ♫

Have you ever had an argument with someone about the best way to do something? You think your way is the best, but your sister thinks her way is better. But then maybe you realize that each of you is right—and you work together to reach your goal!

Something similar actually happened with the hymn "Crown Him with Many Crowns," as strange as that may sound. This very long hymn (it originally had twelve verses!) was written by Matthew Bridges and Godfrey Thring—but not at the same time. Bridges, a Catholic, wrote the first six verses. And then twenty-three years later, Thring, a Protestant, decided that even though he liked the hymn, he wanted to add his own theology to it. And so he wrote six more verses.

Today, variations of the song are found in many different hymnals. Some include all twelve verses, some a combination of verses from Bridges and verses from Thring. But all sing about the glory of God and how He deserves to be crowned with many crowns. The story behind this hymn is an excellent reminder that God can always take a disagreement and turn it into something good.

"CROWN HIM WITH MANY CROWNS"

Matthew Bridges, 1800-1894 and Godfrey Thring, 1823-1903 | George J. Elvey, 1816-1893

Crown Him with man - y crowns, the Lamb up - on the throne; Hark! how the heaven - ly an - them drowns all mu - sic but its own. A - wake, my soul, and sing of Him who died for thee, And hail Him as thy match - less King through all e - ter - ni - ty.

2)

Crown Him the Son of God before the worlds began,

And ye, who tread where He hath trod, crown Him the Son of man;

Who every grief hath known that wrings the human breast,

And takes and bears them for His own, that all in Him may rest.

3)

Crown Him the Lord of life, who triumphed o'er the grave,

And rose victorious in the strife for those He came to save;

His glories now we sing who died, and rose on high,

Who died, eternal life to bring, and lives, that death may die.

4)

Crown Him the Lord of love! Behold His hands and side,

Rich wounds, yet visible above, in beauty glorified;

All hail, Redeemer, hail! For Thou hast died for me:

Thy praise shall never, never fail throughout eternity.

"'TIS SO SWEET TO TRUST IN JESUS"

Trust the Trail Boss

I grew up on a farm where we had lots of horses. I loved to ride my pony behind the bigger horses that my dad and older sisters rode. In single file, we would follow the trail along the Patapsco River, riding the horses through a scenic state park. About a mile into our ride, the river changed course and tumbled over jagged rocks. That's where the trail became a narrow path that twisted and climbed up a steep ledge of rock. On the other side of the river was an alternate trail that led through a flat, grassy meadow.

My sisters always wanted to spur their horses up the dangerous, slippery slope. We had seen other riders race their horses up that ledge like wild cowboys. The danger factor made it seem fun and exciting. Our dad, however, refused to let us do such a reckless thing.

My family had an unspoken rule: My sisters and I had to stick close behind our father, who always rode the lead horse. As trail boss, he had the final say on which trail we would take. With him in charge, it always meant we would take the safer path.

Still, every time we came to that fork in the trail, I would look longingly toward the rocky side of the river. And even though I wanted to try the exciting trail, I'm glad my dad was so firm and wise. It was easy to trust my father because deep down, I knew he was right. I knew he was looking out for our safety. Now whenever I find myself longing to take the path filled with risks—risks that aren't good for me or for those around me—I always remind myself that my heavenly Father is the boss. He has the final say, and it would be foolish to disobey Him or to refuse the path He has chosen for me.

When I think of trusting someone who always wants the best for me, I think of the hymn "'Tis So Sweet to Trust in Jesus." I love to sing it so I can show God how much I completely trust Him. It also reminds me that I am safe when Jesus is in charge and I choose to follow Him. It's so sweet to trust in Jesus because He always knows what's right and what's best for us. ♫

A young girl named Louisa dreamed of becoming a missionary. Her dream eventually came true, and she spent fifteen years on the mission field in South Africa. But little did she know the hard times that would come before she became a missionary.

After Louisa had grown up and married, she and her husband and their four-year-old daughter, Lily, were enjoying a sunny day, eating a picnic lunch on a favorite beach in New York. Suddenly the cheerful day was interrupted by the cries of a young boy who was drowning in the ocean. Louisa's husband rushed into the sea to save the boy, but tragically, both the boy and Louisa's husband were drowned.

Louisa's troubles did not end there. She and Lily were very poor for many years. Louisa never lost her faith in God, but she often asked Him, "Why? Why are these hard things happening to me and my daughter?" She wrote the words to "'Tis So Sweet to Trust in Jesus" to show that joy can always be found in trusting Jesus, no matter what difficult things may happen.

"'TIS SO SWEET TO TRUST IN JESUS"

Louisa M.R. Stead, c. 1850-1917 | William J. Kirkpatrick, 1838-1921

'Tis so sweet to trust in Je-sus, Just to take Him at His word;

Just to rest up-on His pro-mise; Just to know, "Thus saith the Lord."

Je-sus, Je-sus, how I trust Him! How I've proved Him o'er and o'er!

Je-sus, Je-sus, pre-cious Je-sus! O for grace to trust Him more!

2)

O how sweet to trust in Jesus, just to trust His cleansing blood;

Just in simple faith to plunge me 'neath the healing, cleansing flood!

Refrain

Jesus, Jesus, how I trust Him! How I've proved Him o'er and o'er!

Jesus, Jesus, precious Jesus! O for grace to trust Him more!

3)

Yes, 'tis sweet to trust in Jesus, just from sin and self to cease;

Just from Jesus simply taking life and rest and joy and peace.

Refrain

4)

I'm so glad I learned to trust Thee, precious Jesus, Savior, Friend;

And I know that Thou art with me, wilt be with me to the end.

Refrain

"ALL CREATURES OF OUR GOD AND KING"

Praising Our Creator

How do God's creatures praise their Creator? What does it sound like? I always ask myself those questions when I hear the first line of this wonderful hymn: "All creatures of our God and King, lift up your voice and with us sing: Alleluia, alleluia!"

God created human beings to give Him praise. Every single person is wired to worship. And everything else that God created also gives Him glory. Yes, the meadows and the mountains, the oceans and the skies—they all show us what a great Creator God is. But these settings are merely backdrops for more reasons to praise God.

God created insects, fish, butterflies, bullfrogs, and all the other animals to inhabit the mountains, meadows, oceans, and skies—all for the purpose of glorifying Him. Consider the way a peacock struts around, fanning his brilliantly colored tail feathers. Picture a monkey swinging effortlessly from tree to tree, never missing a branch. The next time you go camping in a forest, listen to the chorus of birds singing at sunrise. It's *beautiful*! And God created it all.

When peacocks strut their stuff and monkeys swing in the trees like gymnasts and feathered friends sing their morning melodies, they are giving glory to God. They're being who God created them to be. It's their way of singing, "Alleluia! God made me this way, and I *love* singing and showing off His creativity!" It makes God happy when we enjoy animals and insects and all of His creation "doing their thing." He loves to see us give Him the credit for being their Creator. It's like doubling His glory!

Lions roar and kittens purr. Parakeets sing and orangutans swing. Grizzlies growl and coyotes howl. Butterflies flit and meerkats sit. Fish float and antelopes…well, they *lope*. Kangaroos hippity-hop and worship with sounds you've probably never, ever heard. Every one of God's creatures was designed to reflect the majesty of its Creator—and they are at their happiest when they are doing what God intended them to do. Every creature of our God and King gives Him praise when they talk and move and play. And we can do the same! ♫

Can you imagine growing up in a wealthy household and having everything you ever wanted—but then throwing it all away? That's exactly what Saint Francis of Assisi did. He grew up in luxury but felt God calling him to a life of poverty. And so he began to wander from place to place, walking barefoot and dressed in rags, as he preached the love of God and composed verses about His goodness.

Saint Francis slept in fields and caves and shared God's message of love and joy with anyone who would listen. Sometimes he even found himself preaching to a flock of birds! He told the birds that God had given them beautiful feathers for clothing and a cheerful voice—and that they should sing and praise Him.

The hymn "All Creatures of Our God and King" is taken from a poem he wrote called "Canticle of the Sun." A man named William Henry Draper translated the words from Italian to English, and the hymn was joyfully sung for the first time at a children's festival. Quite possibly the birds joined the children as they sang their praise to God!

"ALL CREATURES OF OUR GOD AND KING"

Francis of Assisi, 1182-1226, translation by William H. Draper, 1855-1933 | German hymn tune

All crea-tures of our God and King, Lift up your voice and with us sing Al-le-

lu ia! Al-le-lu – ia! Thou burn-ing sun with gold-en beam, Thou

sil-ver moon with soft-er gleam! O praise Him, O praise Him! Al-le-

lu – ia! Al-le-lu – ia! Al-le-lu – – ia!

2)

Thou rushing wind that art so strong,

Ye clouds that sail in heav'n along, O praise Him! Alleluia!

Thou rising morn, in praise rejoice,

Ye lights of evening, find a voice!

O praise Him, O praise Him! Alleluia! Alleluia! Alleluia!

3)

And all ye men of tender heart,

Forgiving others, take your part, O sing ye! Alleluia!

Ye who long pain and sorrow bear,

Praise God and on Him cast your care!

O praise Him, O praise Him! Alleluia! Alleluia! Alleluia!

4)

Let all things their Creator bless,

And worship Him in humbleness, O praise Him! Alleluia!

Praise, praise the Father, praise the Son,

And praise the Spirit, Three in One!

O praise Him, O praise Him! Alleluia! Alleluia! Alleluia!

"HOW GREAT THOU ART"

Embracing the Adventure

I once went on an ocean cruise with my grandmother. The first morning of our trip, the sky was cloudy, and the ocean was churning with whitecapped waves. A fierce wind and rain kept most of the passengers indoors and away from the deck. My grandmother, wanting us to stay inside, took me to watch a slide presentation about ocean currents.

Like most kids, I found it really hard to sit in a warm, dark room and listen to the click-clacking of the machine as it projected one slide after the next. Restlessly I squirmed in my seat. Why couldn't I be outside standing on the wet deck, holding on to the railing while turning my face to the wind and salt spray? Who thought it would be a good idea to learn about ocean currents inside a stuffy, dark room when we could be experiencing the ocean's power firsthand?

Later that day, my grandmother wrapped me in a coat and scarf and took me outside onto the deck. We reached for the ship's railing to steady ourselves as the big vessel tilted. Enthralled by a sense of danger and adventure, we faced the wild waves and the whipping wind. As the wind blew fiercely, I gripped the rail tighter, awestruck by the majesty and power of the ocean.

I imagine us worshipping God in the same way I experienced the power of the ocean. Yes, Jesus can be safe and comforting, but following Him is also a journey full of excitement and adventure. God is awesome, and we take a risk when we choose to follow Him. Following Him should be like standing in front of a powerful storm, throwing your arms wide, and shouting out with all your heart, "God, I'm ready to live my life for You!"

You already know what it feels like to marvel at something like the mighty ocean or a massive thunderstorm or a sky filled with unbelievably bright stars. When you choose to follow Jesus, prepare to be blown away by His love and grace and power. The more time you spend in His presence, the more you will learn about Him and the more you will become like Him. You'll experience His greatness and awesomeness, and you'll live a life of excitement and adventure. ♫

Have you ever been playing outside when it started to rain or even thunder and lightning? You probably ran home as fast as you could! The same thing happened to a man named Carl Boberg when he was walking home from church in Sweden. He was listening to the church bells and enjoying the beautiful day when a sudden storm appeared. Loud claps of thunder and brilliant streaks of lightning followed by torrential rain made Carl hurry home!

As quickly as it had appeared, the sudden storm disappeared. At home, Carl opened wide the windows of his house to let in the fresh air and saw a beautiful rainbow. He was so inspired by his experience that he immediately wrote a poem about it. This poem talks all about God's power and how He shows Himself to us through His amazing creation.

Years later, Stuart Hine heard the poem being sung in Russian. Stuart adapted the words and melody, and the hymn became known as "How Great Thou Art." Followers of God throughout Europe, Africa, Asia, and the Americas have learned its tune and sung its words, praising God for His awesome power and might.

HOW GREAT THOU ART

Stuart K. Hine, 1899-1989 | Swedish folk melody, adapted and arranged by Stuart K. Hine

O Lord my God! When I in awe - some won - der Con - sid - er all the worlds Thy hands have made, I see the stars, I hear the roll - ing thun - der, Thy power through - out the un - i - verse dis - played, Then sings my soul, my Sav - ior God to Thee; How great Thou art, how great Thou art! Then sings my soul, my Sav - ior God to Thee; How great Thou art, how great Thou art!

2)

When through the woods and forest glades I wander
And hear the birds sing sweetly in the trees,
When I look down from lofty mountain grandeur,
And hear the brook and feel the gentle breeze:

Refrain
Then sings my soul, my Savior God, to Thee:
How great Thou art! How great Thou art!
Then sings my soul, my Savior God, to Thee:
How great Thou art! How great Thou art!

3)

And when I think that God, His Son not sparing,
Sent Him to die, I scarce can take it in,
That on the cross, my burden gladly bearing,
He bled and died to take away my sin.

Refrain

4)

When Christ shall come with shout of acclamation
And take me home, what joy shall fill my heart!
Then I shall bow in humble adoration,
And there proclaim, "My God, how great Thou art!"

Refrain

"PRAISE GOD, FROM WHOM ALL BLESSINGS FLOW"

Father, Son, and Holy Spirit

God is so much bigger than our minds can ever grasp! This is why I love to pray large prayers to Him. I even start my prayers large. I'll begin by saying, "Oh, wonderful Father, precious Jesus, and blessed Holy Spirit, thank You for listening to my prayer." Praying this way reminds me of the last line of this hymn, which is often called the Doxology: "Praise Father, Son and Holy Ghost, Amen!"

Let's explore each Person mentioned in that last line of the Doxology. First, let's look at the Father. He is especially wonderful because God the Father's special gift to us is His plan of salvation. The Father was the one who came up with the idea of saving sinful people. We would have been lost for eternity were it not for our heavenly Father's plan to rescue us. And so we need to worship Him with great respect.

Next, there's God the Son and the special gift of grace He gives to us. Jesus is the one who followed through on the Father's plan of salvation. He obeyed His heavenly Father by going to the cross to die for our sins. Because of this, we need to show we are grateful that Jesus obeyed His Father. By obeying, Jesus became our Savior.

Finally, there's the Holy Spirit. (A long time ago, people used to call the Holy Spirit the Holy Ghost.) When I think about the Holy Spirit and His gifts of strength and encouragement, I remember that He's the one who gives us assurance and joy. That's why we should be careful to listen to Him. We don't want to make Him sad, upset Him, or stifle His voice by disobeying Him.

Father, Son, and Holy Spirit. The Doxology is a wonderful way to praise God in all His fullness. When we sing the words to this hymn, we are expressing how wide, long, high, and deep the love of God really is. And we are sharing the good news of how God desires to fill us to the brim with His fullness of love. Isn't that awesome? So think large and gladly say with me, "Father, Son, and Holy Spirit...I worship You." ♫

Did you know that a song that was originally sung only in secret would one day become the most-sung hymn in the world? That's what happened with "Praise God from Whom All Blessings Flow."

Thomas Ken, who wrote this wonderful hymn, was orphaned as a child and raised by his sister, Anne, and her author husband, Izaak Walton. Thomas became a poet and pastor who wrote this simple song of praise for the students he taught at Winchester College in England. The students loved the song, but Ken warned them that they should only sing it in the privacy of their dorm rooms. At that time, the church believed that songs should only include the words of Scripture verses, not the writer's own ideas and feelings.

Fortunately, many people continued to sing the song, and eventually the church decided it was okay for songs to include the words of their writers—especially beautiful songs of praise like the Doxology. In fact, today many churches have a tradition of ending their services with this hymn that was once only sung in secret behind closed doors!

PRAISE GOD, FROM WHOM ALL BLESSINGS FLOW

Thomas Ken, 1637–1711 | Louis Bourgeois, c. 1510–1561

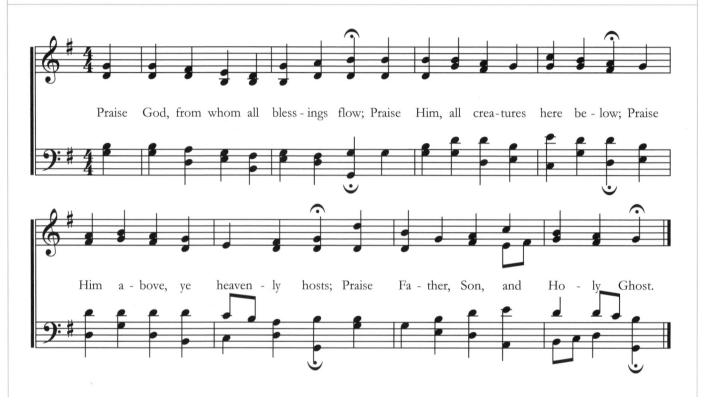

Praise God, from whom all bless-ings flow; Praise Him, all crea-tures here be-low; Praise

Him a-bove, ye heaven-ly hosts; Praise Fa-ther, Son, and Ho-ly Ghost.

> Teach and admonish one another with all wisdom through psalms, hymns, and songs from the Spirit, singing to God with gratitude in your hearts.
>
> Colossians 3:16

Sing to the LORD a new song;

sing to the LORD, all the earth.

Sing to the LORD, praise his name;

proclaim his salvation day after day.

PSALM 96:1-2

Joni Eareckson Tada is a gifted artist and author as well as an international advocate for people with disabilities. A quadriplegic since the age of 17, she has written bestselling and award-winning works on topics ranging from disability outreach to reaching out to God. Joni and her husband, Ken, call California home.

Bobbie Wolgemuth was a Bible teacher and the author or coauthor of several books, including the notes to *Mom's Bible*. She was married to Robert Wolgemuth for 35 years, and together they had two married daughters, two sons-in-law, and five grandchildren. Bobbie went to be with the Lord on October 28, 2014, after a brave battle with cancer.

Yuris Yoon is a wife and mother, saved by the unending grace of God. When she's not chasing around the kids, Yuris runs Salt Stains, an online art print shop inspired by God's beautiful creation.